Aflame but Unconsumed

Aflame but Unconsumed

Poems by

Timothy E. G. Bartel

© 2019 Timothy E. G. Bartel. All rights reserved.
This material may not be reproduced in any form,
published, reprinted, recorded, performed, broadcast,
rewritten or redistributed without the explicit permission
of Timothy E. G. Bartel.
All such actions are strictly prohibited by law.

Cover design by Shay Culligan

ISBN: 978-1-950462-06-3

Kelsay Books Inc.

kelsaybooks.com
502 S 1040 E
A119
American Fork, Utah
84003

For my students

an American sonnet ... a little room in a house set aflame

—Terrance Hayes

Acknowledgments

Thanks are in order to the following periodicals:

Christendom Review: "The Apologia of Abdiel," "Julian the Apostate in Athens," "Things You Can Do with Ideas"

The Cressett: "Willard"

Curator Magazine: "Handset," "Hymn on Bow Making," "Lazarus," "Remembering"

Pointed Circle: "The Ruins"

Shantih Journal: "Amendment 1," "Soviet Fall"

Transpositions: "Palm to Palm," "The Cross above St. John's"

Windhover Journal: "November 1"

Contents

I. Abdiel

Handset	15
The *Apologia* of Abdiel	16
The Cross above St John's	17
Julian the Apostate in Athens[1]	18
Hymn to the Early Christian Poets[2]	20
ISIS in Mosul	21
Hymn to Zaha Hadid	24
Things You Can Do with Ideas:	26
Hymn on Bow Making	27
On Children	28
Palm to Palm	29
Remembering	30

II. A Habit for the Autumn

Soviet Fall	33
November 1	34
St Ephrem's Reply	35
Amendment 1	36
Lazarus	37
Incumbent	38
November 8	39
Willard	40
On Anxiety	41
Advent	42
Paradigm Shift	43
The Story	44
The Limits of Empiricism	45
The New Gregorian	46
December	47
Hymn on Craft	48

I.

Abdiel

The flaming Seraph fearless, though alone
Encompassed round with foes, thus answered bold.
—Milton, *Paradise Lost* V.875–876

Handset

The poem is unlocked. No brand   can block her.
And her only limitations   in data and in
Generation are   the words you know. So—

What games or searches   shall we undertake?
The victories and answers we   might end with
Cost a lifetime, take   no bandwidth.

The *Apologia* of Abdiel

is found in book five   of *Paradise Lost,*
when Satan calls his   followers to mass
against the tyranny of God   and just one punk named
Abdiel defies   Satan to his face
then flies fast southward   back to sanity.
I too would like to   stage revolt
against the demons   in my north
where passions pack like   seven days of snow.

What nerve or immaterial strain   induces spirits
to rebel against   that old rebellion
in the welling chest?   This warm afternoon
it's past time for me   to imitate some
insolent,   God re-praising deed.

The Cross above St John's

Santa Fe, 2007

There was the long, white, welded cross
Lying on the hilltop above the pines.
How had it fallen? Surely not by wind
Alone. Rust, perhaps? Then the bigger questions:
Could I pick it up? Stand it back upright?
I will make a poem of this, I thought:
Raising again the long, white, welded cross.

It proved (for crosses can admit of proof,
I learned), quite difficult to lift—
Impossible. I couldn't even get
The transept to my shoulders so to re-
Enact the part of Simon of Cyrene.
I think I only helped to move
It further down the hill.

I reasoned with myself that this may be
Best after all: the cross, I saw, had snapped
Off from its base, as if from some intentioned
Act of bending it past breaking. Even
If I could have lifted, how to re-secure
It to its broken base? No. Let it lie.
Brown thunder-clouds were crowding afternoon.

Still I lingered, sad I could not make
A poem of it. Still its broken base—
Among some scattered granite—gaped. A cross
Belonged there once; and so I found some twine
And wrapped two boughs of Mexican scrub pine
Till they stood cruciform above the hill
Propped up in stones I gathered with my hands.

Julian the Apostate in Athens[1]

AD 355

Good riddance, then—return to Cappadocia,
My Christian friends, who came to Athens proud
Of your new freedom unlocked at Milan,
Where Constantine threw wide the doors of Rome
To welcome in the doctrines of the East
Where God and man flash between sky and earth.
All this our cults could take if not for law—
And moral law at that—which echoes from
Such lighting landings and such lightning leavings
Like throbs of thunder that can shatter glass.
Jove jumped to earth a thousand times, but placed
No shackles on my conduct or my mind;
Now this new Jove, this Jesus, throws not bolts
But new commandments, striking men to earth
And soon all Rome will groan under his crush.
The provinces may buckle, the whole world
Yield then to his unyielding creed until
This dusty grove at Athens, this Academy
Will close its ancient doors—of mind—
And be transformed into another ruin where
The enemies of Christ lie lifeless.
                                            No.
There is another god still in the earth,
But slumbering till his prophet cries, "Awake!"
Awake, then, Janus, lord of doors and years,
And make this heart of mine conservative.
Come, too, Eumenides, who haunt these hearths
And gather round me like a laurel crown—
I come to lend you back a little of
The wrath that great Athena leached from you;
For I know where the greatest matricides
Reside: in Galilee, where Roman sons

Have left the pantheon that nursed them when
The slim sinews of reason had not formed,
And humans were a myth that death composed.
I, backed by Chaos, ringed by Fury, I
Will raise the brazen scepter; will turn back
The swift horse of imperial time; will ride,
When it is mine, the promised throne like some
High ship's Octavian prow to Galilee,
Jerusalem, to Rome—wherever that
Malignant cross has burned a mark—
And exorcise Jehovah from my home.

But look—the olives here are still pale red,
And spring and youth still cling within the trees.
This earth, for now, for all, will be enough.
We pagan men are humble, not too humble;
We do not wish for immortality,
The flame that should, by right, belong to gods.
I will be happy if my name lives on.
I ask no other privilege. Resurrection
Is a prideful hope, a vain one too.
The gods did not become men so we could
Become as gods ourselves—we are more mild.
For men are a myth created by Death,
Brief stories told by changing time's moonlight,
And all who overreach their natures will
Be overthrown, as oceans toss a child.

Hymn to the Early Christian Poets[2]

We are selfish men;
Oh! raise us up, return to us again;
And give us manners, virtue, freedom, power.
          —Wordsworth, to Milton

You early Christian poets, slight
In even critics' memories,
Who wrote illegal hymns in Rome
Or paired your lines in Antioch

As David did down south: first thought
Rethought, re-spoken in the next
Verset, then passed from lips to ears
To chant in flame-licked catacombs,

Or publish in the public air,
Disguising Christ in anapests
As fish or lamb or bridled colt,
Or phoenix in the rising flame.

And when Milan came, you were posed
Already to enact a change
Within the echelons of verse:
You reached your careful lines to bridge

The gulf between Rome's seven hills
And those high cliffs of Zion where
The unnamed God once spoke with man.
We need you now, your unashamed

Devotion and your dual mistrust
Of outer drift and inner urge,
Your bold insistence that the soul
Is no less stubborn than the flesh.

ISIS in Mosul

1. How to Destroy a Relic

Mosque of the Prophet Jonah, Mosul, Summer 2014

You first must find the quiet place within
The mosque or church where it resides;
Take Jonah's shrine: a little chapel where
Among dry flower-buds he waits inside
A peaked and concrete tomb enameled with
The blue of seas where whales gulp and spew.
Now close the door, but let your right hand know
Your left hand brought a hammer, long and sledge.

A sideways swing is best for a beginning—
Now pound upon that blue and ancient tomb
Until you cannot tell where rubble ends
And where his bones begin. To really put
A seal upon your morning's work, run clear
And detonate the hated house of prayer.

2. The Masked Iraqi

Photograph taken just before the storming of Eastern Mosul, Fall 2016

I want to know and cannot know his name,
This soldier with a half-skull mask: he stands
Against a scape of faded buildings, on
His chest a poly vest, all hung with tools:
Thin, wire cutting scissors, red-orange flares,
And rifle clips, once white, worn to dull shine.
His helmet, black and dusted, has a frame
In which to place a rank or name: it's blank.

I read he marches to free Mosul soon,
And think of Jonah, too, who entered there
Conflicted that it must be he to go,
But still intent on seeing justice done.
The Ninevites put ash and sackcloth on
To hear the God's rebuke. And Jonah withered.

3. The Ruins

Western Mosul, Spring 2017

The coalition soldiers pause before
The bomb-crushed building—wires slag like moss
On sloping heaps of concrete, meters deep.
How many living breathe beneath? Who called
The US air-strike that has pierced the walls
With missiles? For no terrorists were there:
Just families, just locals shunning war.
The Western powers shift in cramping seats,
Reorganize their papers, make a call
To open an investigation. Still
Each coalition soldier stands, as if
He were a faceless statue. Blocks beyond
Another boy builds bombs. New whimpers rise
From underneath the unforgiving ruins.

Hymn to Zaha Hadid

1950–2016

Until your craft, Iraq did not
Mean architecture to the world.
It meant Saddam, or oil, or war,
Or Western intervention's wrongs.

You made it mean prisms of glass,
And buildings posed like water-scooped
Obsidian in civic streams.
Let critics curse the arc of art

Away from forms that men once loved:
You gave us shapes to reckon our
Oblique and bending bodies with:
Glaswegian roofs of steel bent like

A heart-beat peak, and in Beijing
Redented office towers curved
Like Angkor Wat in glass and steel
Which tempt a few to worship there

Where every level gently lifts
The eyes another rank toward sky
And buildings all around them seem
A stack of flat, unyielding planes.

Organic form—the aim of craft
For Morris and for Wright—has paused
And lingered in your work, as birds
Will duck beneath a stream, then fling

The beading water up into
Expectant air from oily wings.
Some aspect of those beads, that oil,
You cast across this crowded earth

Before your death, when Baghdad strove
With ISIS for control of what
Iraq's new shape would be, and your
Eccentric heartbeat ceased to peak.

Things You Can Do with Ideas:

Treasure them like mint condition comics;
Hide them from your sister till she weeps.
Cut them into pieces; paste them next
To favorite passages in books you read.
Bury your ideas in the earth,
Shoot them into space in some slim rocket,
Pave the road with them as if they're concrete,
Fill your ribcage with them like they're air,
Or sit in some dark room and feel them pulse
Out from you into nothing, separate
And slip away. Your mind will quiet for
A summer moment.
                        Then they will
Return, now sevenfold, and make you more
A servant of themselves than when they left.

Hymn on Bow Making

But when you are fed up with it,
This buying what another made,
You walk into your own backyard
And scan the trees for straight, thin limbs.

Once found, you cut one down, or two,
And let it hang a while above
Your dryer, so its sap can set
Within it, lose liquidity

And harden 'til it is a match
For knife-blades or the bite of planes.
And then the shaping—hatchet first,
To peel off quick the bark and thick

Of bow-back, then the finer work
With whittling knife to balance, shave,
And thin. And last, the sanding with
A thicker grit that fills the air

With dust of what was living wood.
You have, if you have been a bold
And careful carpenter, a bow
To string with that respect that comes

From knowing that at any time
All that you've set your crafting to
May snap to useless pieces in
Your hands. So art is; so is life,

And so is every single bow
You make, success no guarantee
That next time you are truly brave
You will not fail, or find a greater foe.

On Children

To help them sleep is a creative act:
You choose what seems a fitting setting: bed.
You plot a structure: prayers, then lullaby,
Then slowly slowing down the tune until
It could be breathing just as soon as song,
Then creeping, often on your hands and knees,
While listening intently to their breath,
Back through the evening darkness toward the door.

So many things can cause your form to break:
A sudden thirst, the question why we die,
Or how we're born, or why we chose to eat
A salad dinner when we could have cake.
Most often, though, it seems so random why,
When all has been made ready, they still wake.

Palm to Palm

For my wife

We are the two hands of the sentinel
Who paces wakeful in the windless night,
Attentive to each whimpered sigh. We know
The drying of the sleepless eyes, the light
Delirium of rising to attend
To late disturbances in humid air
And midnight panics. We are hands, I say
That grip the issued rifle of close care.

It's years since I first chose this martial art:
To clasp and interdigitate, to match,
As best I can, your grip with mine—we part
But to extend our reach, and meet again.
The weary heat of each of us is cooled
By droplets from the other's giving skin.

Remembering

First, too much play would cause the crotch-tab to
Break off; the thumb was often the next part
To crack when holding weapons stressed its glue—
And last, the band which joined the hips to heart
Snapped. Then I'd have two halves of G.I. Joe.
I find a bag of partial figures, toys
Which waited twenty years for me to grow
Until tonight, when I, no longer boy,

Now lay them out in pieces to be pressed
Back whole. I find the hook between the legs,
And, using a screwdriver's tip, I thread
A gleaming ring from hook to spine. A chest
Can hold that all in place. I dust the face,
Commence the reattachment of the head.

II.

A Habit for the Autumn

Thus you may justly wonder why I write at all.
With measured labor—first—I discipline my soul,
For writing lines can order my unmetered mind
And keep my greedy pen in check; instead I spend
My sweat on metric form.

—Gregory Nazianzus, "On the Metered," ll. 28–32

Soviet Fall

November begins with a dream of storm,
Of cloud escarpments in a crowded sky,
And rolling gusts of bone-grey dust. The world
Would end like that, we guessed: a ring of cloud
Expanding from some central flash, then ash.
Our cowed imagination's favorite fear
Was thus when that enormous bear could fuss
And trouble from the east.
                           The bear is joined
By borderless menageries of beasts,
And now we doubt how it will end. There is
No desk to duck within or window to
Avoid. So I will court the apertures
And seats beside their light. Since death will come
For all, I'll sit where it is wide and bright.

November 1

All saints today—not just this martyr who
Expired in boiling oil, or that nun
Who wrote her hymns in peaceful age, but all.
Not Margaret only, Nicholas, or Anne,
But also nameless hosts of faithful boys
Beheaded in the desert, holy girls
Sold into slavery who made their stand
Of protest on the porch of pagan temples;
Not only they, but all.
       How do you make
Yourself prepared for such a feast? Admit
Your frailty: none could properly maintain
Full veneration to an unknown host.
You only can participate—try on
A habit for the autumn, or for life.

St Ephrem's Reply

"The woman in the story did succumb
And eat the fruit forbidden by her Lord,
But was it not a woman also who
Said yes to Gabriel when he came down
To find a willing mother for his God?
Was it not Mary, Mary Magdalene,
Joanna, and Susanna who first saw
Christ's empty tomb and first proclaimed it to
The male disciples cowering in the dawn?"

So Ephrem answered when the skeptical
Had asked why he would form a women's choir,
To chant *madrases* boldly while the priests
And bishops listened, silent and alert
Below the muted icons of the twelve.

Amendment 1

The freest speech takes longest to be freed.
It waits where it is sure it must belong,
In mental realms undredged by common thought
Like glowing fish in trenches miles down,
Unlit by sun, unclassified by eyes.
But glow they do, the self-illumined things,
Among the massive shadows of the deep,
Their power sensed in stillness or in sleep.

I do not know the deepest speech in me;
It may be anger, madness, or a song
That waits beyond the bitterness of years.
Be patient with the one who measures out
And casts another line into herself:
The freest speech takes longest to be freed.

Lazarus

One sonnet can imbue a history
With upright strength when shouted prose demands
It bow to fear or riches. Emma writes
Though publishers refuse her name in print,
Though civil rights do not include her vote,
Though literati fear that Jewish friends
Will taint their reputation, Emma writes.
She writes a sonnet for the statue-gift,

And crafts a climax that the immigrant
Will need to hear, will recognize as mirror:
"Your poor, your tired, your huddled"—these her blood
Knows like an heirloom—so she smiths a key
To foil the forces in each age that shrink
Before the stranger, lock the golden door.

Incumbent

The changing circumstance of power chafes
Resolve in each executive until
He hates that he was placed in charge and hates
The power that he holds. So sickness is
The norm of the administrative state,
And bodies politic harbor disease
Where most would hope for youth and strength.
Such wisdom comes with time to all who lead.

Come see the early-graying heads of state;
Distrust the ones with hope still in their eyes—
They have not yet been ripened by slow time.
Now see the whitened former heads of state
Who make their rest a resignation to
The ache of aging wounds, hopeless of balm.

November 8

Just one more week till Advent, when the soul
Begins to bend toward Christmas, when the wait
Begins in earnest, short days at a time,
And long nights filled with tail-lights and rain.
My mind twists north, to Market Street in fall
Where pavement stones perform the bite
And slip of frost on shoe, and little cars
Park shivering at each curb, huddled with life.

It's warmer here in my November south:
The trees are in denial that their leaves
Are less thick than a month ago. The streets
Still hoard their monsoon mud along each curb.
Some FM, prematurely cranked up loud
Belts "Come thou long expected" down the street.

Willard

Within a holy mystery of sense
We see contingency as precious: one
Misplaces key, or phone, or grocery list
And, wanting it in urgency, with strong
Imagination feels it in one's grip,
And almost can be baffled wishing did
Not make the thing appear. It was just here,
And mind rebukes it for its disobeying.

I have an inkling death is similar:
One loses hold on what is hard and sure,
And spins in bafflement. My father says
That as my grand-dad died, he jerked awake,
And asked in panic where it was: that thing
That had been in his hands, and now was gone.

On Anxiety

The tense tectonics of a life surprise
Us when they shift, and the foundation grout
Of love, belief, and habit grinds to dust.
The stresses that can set the quaking off
Seem incommensurate with what falls down.
How few commitments really were fixed fast:
Delight in one's career, a patient love
Of spouse or child, a vow to never harm.

My lover, you release me with a breath,
And all my continents unhinge from spheres—
You gather them, my planes and angles, teach
Them laws of symmetry, relations that
Are fruitful. Lips against my ear, you ground
With gentle skin what trembles most in me.

Advent

The rain today is herald of December;
The little drops that cling and drip from brick
Are recapitulations of the lights
That yesterday my neighbor stretched and tacked
Along his eaves. He kneeled on his roof
Attentive to its pitch and shift amid
The humid evening air, his stubbled sweat
Performing its own feat of clinging on.

The light can only shine through what is clear:
The glass of bulbs, the bulge of water drops,
The unpolluted sky, the aetherless
Expanse of space untaught by any laws
Of atmosphere. There starlight slaloms down
The ancient slopes of spheres to winter here.

Paradigm Shift

The vogue of relativity expires
A hundred years since it was first proposed
By self-correcting Einstein. In that age
The mass of many worlds shaped space itself,
And thrilled researchers cast equations out
To catch the fickle vectors of the light
Which slid through tight topographies of time,
Now bulged and now bisected by the spheres.

What model of a cosmos would you have:
A fun-house mirror bent by heaving suns?
A vast cathedral stacked from quantum cubes
Like depth-stretched pixels on a plane? Or else
A haunted wood, where chaos gapes below
The questing girl, and old gods lust above?

The Story

The story is a girl in the woods.
She holds a hatchet in her hand and in
Her mind she holds a knowledge of the woods
Like several precious coins too dear to spend
On trinkets. She is looking from the trees
Into a space beyond, where those woods end.
A road begins there that will lead past hills
Until it finds a city in decline
Where art is decadent and civil laws
Are all subservient to changing norms.
The story is the girl setting out,
The hatchet on her belt and in her mind
Her knowledge of the woods like few gold coins
Too precious to be spent on any good.

The Limits of Empiricism

Experiments must end in guess or doubt,
But never certainly a yes or no.
The seasoned scientist stands half convinced
Before repeated trials with matched results.
Still, probable wins over possible:
The rocket lifts the ship, the gears propel
The axle, medication calms the ache,
And further stimulus improves the Dow.

The best I hope to do is cultivate
A habit for the autumn, kindling frames
Where interest and invention meet in me.
Where is the shining, lasting, concrete thing,
To hitch a culture or a life onto?
Look for a craft aflame but unconsumed.

The New Gregorian

A brief poetics takes into account
Four spheres of audience: the untrained self
That in the act of making finds a curb
And meter that it may yet imitate;
The church is next, the fold you find yourself
Within, who most accept whatever's said,
And you who say it; after that the world,
The reading culture of your vulgar age,

Where worldviews are hurled and genres crushed,
And undiminished fame is gained by none;
The final audience? Your soul, at death.
What have you crafted that could aid her in
Her journey on? In brief, you must account
For each each time you write. Heed most the last.

December

Again the wreath, again the tree, again
The memory of Tennyson. Again
The sharp anticipation in the heart
That drives us all through time into the dark—
Dark wall against late dawn, dark wall against
The afternoon: they cramp the thinning light
While night spreads wide her arms to let the stars
Rest long upon on her ever-velvet chest.

The stars grow weak from flaming in the black,
Their only company the spheres that, dim,
Bounce lonely stars their faint reflections back.
Beyond them there is no created thing,
But tons of quantum lack, and One that waits
Unmade beyond the bulk of even that.

Hymn on Craft

Each autumn calls me back to craft,
To those old terms: attention, work,
The whittling down, the filling out,
The wondering if it is worth

The time I dedicate to it.
The poet balancing her lines,
Or architect with compass poised
To draft an angle so her joist

Will fit within the thinning space
Between the ruin and the apt,
Or she who dedicates long hours
To training little boughs to bend

As if blown west by steady breeze
Though they grow on a bonsai in
A glass and windless gallery:
These all can seem such trifled types.

But every life must find its work;
Some spend their years in making laws
Some making money, others homes,
And some have chosen time a fit

Dimension for a feat with words:
To shape a story into beats
That match the unheard rhythm of
The deep and chambered human heart.

The worth of this will have to wait
For that proposed dimension of
Eternity to be revealed.
Each fall I make a wager with

Whatever god has made the waves
That if they move in measure with
The moon, then there is something worth
In work that imitates the metered world.

Notes

1. The Emperor Julian ruled the Roman Empire from 361 to 363 AD. In a fascinating coincidence of history, Julian attended the Academy at Athens in 355 AD alongside two of the great Christian theologians of the fourth century, St Basil of Caesarea and St Gregory of Nazianzus. But in Athens, Julian committed himself not to the Christian faith, as his predecessor Constantine and his schoolmates had done, but instead to Greco-Roman paganism. He is often called "the Apostate" for his persecution of Christians during his rule.

2. This and the other hymns in this collection are written in the fourth century Ambrosian hymn form. This form was invented by St Ambrose of Milan and consists of unrhymed quatrains of iambic tetrameter, often 8 stanzas in all. These hymns originally celebrated a religious event or figure, and were used in both communal worship and political protest.

About the Author

Timothy E. G. Bartel is a poet and professor from California. His poems have appeared in *Christianity and Literature*, *Saint Katherine Review*, and *The Scotsman*, and his chapbook *Arroyos: Sijo and Other Poems*, was named a Book of 2015 by the Scottish Poetry Library. Timothy currently teaches writing at the College at Saint Constantine and hosts the Poetry Corner Podcast.

www.ingramcontent.com/pod-product-compliance
Lightning Source LLC
Chambersburg PA
CBHW021028090426
42738CB00007B/935